Beginning the Journey

Initial Meditation Instructions
Using the Buddha's Map

Doug Kraft

Blue Dolphin Publishing

Published by Blue Dolphin Publishing, Inc.
P O Box 8, Nevada City, CA 95959
Orders 1 800 643-0765
Please call for quantity discounts

Web: www.bluedolphinpublishing.com

ISBN: 978-1-57733-289-3 paperback
ISBN: 978-1-57733-464-4 e-book

Library of Congress Control Number: 2014948217

Portions of this text were modified from chapters 2 and 10 of *Buddha's Map: His Original Teachings on Awakening, Ease, and Insight in the Heart of Meditation,* a book by Doug Kraft (Blue Dolphin Publishing, 2013).

www.dougkraft.com

Printed in the United States of America

5   4   3   2   1

In gratitude to my teachers, especially

Bhante Vimalaramsi

and

John Travis

Table of Contents

Introduction 1

Preparation 2

Yourself 3

Spiritual Friend 4

Light, Expansive, Uplifted 6

Joy 8

The Six Rs 9

Continuity 12

Impersonal 13

Awareness is Magic 16

Buddha's Map 18

Teaspoon of Salt 19

Resources 21

Introduction

This booklet offers the basic meditation instructions described by the Buddha in the earliest records of his talks (as compared to later commentaries on those talks).

If you are new to meditation or considering switching to this style, you'll find all you need to get started. If you are practicing this way already, it may help you review and fine-tune your practice.

On the other hand, if you are seeking a deeper understanding of how the practice works, descriptions of insights that arise out of it, or ways to modify your meditation as it deepens, those are beyond the scope of this small book. *Buddha's Map: His Original Teachings on Awakening, Ease, and Insight in the Heart of Meditation*[1] provides that information in depth and detail. *Breath of Love*[2] and *Moving Dhamma*[3] also offer skillful guidance from my teacher, Bhante Vimalaraṁsi.

The purpose of this booklet is to help you begin walking the Buddha's path of kindness and wisdom.

---

1 Doug Kraft (Blue Dolphin Publishing, 2013).
2 Bhante Vimalaraṁsi (Ehipassiko Foundation, Indonesia, 2012).
3 Bhante Vimalaraṁsi (Dhamma Sukha Meditation Center, 2012).

1

Preparation

Before meditating, it is helpful to find a relatively quiet place to sit comfortably. Sit upright if possible. Lounging invites the body and mind to go to sleep rather than wake up. But the posture should be relaxed. Cushions or chairs are both fine. Sitting cross-legged isn't required. A posture that is familiar to your body will be less distracting and more helpful than one that is uncomfortable.

Next, remember the feeling of happiness or contentment. Perhaps you recently accomplished something that left you feeling great. Perhaps it was the softer happiness of holding a small animal that cuddled into you. Perhaps it was the selfless joy of watching a child play. Perhaps it was the serenity of watching a sunset by the ocean.

All of us have felt happy at times—probably many times in our lives. The feeling may vary depending on temperament, history, conditioning, and circumstance. The flavor of happiness is not important, but the feeling is.

Happiness is where this meditation practice begins—not the memory of the happy situation but the feeling itself. It's like a glowing in the center of your chest.

Yourself

Now put yourself in your heart. Some people visualize easily. Others don't. It's not important that you clearly visualize. Just imagine holding yourself in the center of your chest.

Then send yourself a wish for happiness or well-being: "May I be happy." "May I be peaceful." "May I feel safe and secure." "May I feel ease throughout my day." Any uplifted state is fine.

The phrases are a way of priming the pump—they evoke the uplifted feeling. As it arises, shift your attention to the feeling itself.

Sooner or later the feeling will fade. When it does, repeat a phrase. It's not helpful to repeat it rapidly. That makes the phrase feel mechanical. Rather, say it sincerely, and rest for a few moments with the feeling it evokes. When the feeling wanes, repeat a phrase again.

As you do this, three things arise in the mind-heart:[4] the person to whom you are wishing happiness (yourself), the mental phrase, and the feeling. About 75 percent of your attention should be on the feeling, 20 percent on the person (yourself), and just a little on the phrase used to evoke the feeling.

---

4 In the Pāli language used to record the Buddha's talks, there is no distinction between mind and heart. They are considered a unified quality—mind-heart—rather than separated entities—mind and heart.

Spiritual Friend

After about ten minutes, switch the person to whom you are sending kind wishes. Rather than sending loving kindness to yourself, send it to a "spiritual friend."

A spiritual friend is a living person to whom you find it very easy to wish the best. It might be a favorite teacher or counselor who always has your highest interests at heart. It might be an aunt or uncle who looked out for you. It might be a friend who always has your back.

A partner is not a good choice for a spiritual friend. You may have a lot of love for him or her. But primary relationships are usually complex. For the purposes of meditation, simple is better. For the same reason, a teenage son or daughter is not a good choice—those relationships have too many textures. A person you find physically attractive is not a good choice either. Physical attraction can become thick, complicated, and distracting. Traditionally a spiritual friend is of the gender to which you are less likely to feel sexual attraction. You want the meditation to be light, easy, and uncomplicated.

Once you have settled on a good spiritual friend, stay with that person. As the practice deepens, the instruction will change.[5] But for now, it is best to stay with the same friend. If you switch from one person to another, the practice won't ripen or deepen as easily. If you stay with one person in meditation, the kindness

---

5 Kraft, *Buddha's Map: His Original Teachings on Awakening, Ease, and Insight in the Heart of Meditation,* 191.

4

and ease within you will become stronger. The other people around you will benefit even though they are not the explicit focus of your sitting practice.

Each time you sit down to practice, send well-wishes to yourself for about ten minutes. Then switch to your one chosen spiritual friend.

Light, Expansive, Uplifted

The Buddha talked about four qualities of mind-heart that are particularly wholesome. "Wholesome" means they have very little tension in them or they reduce tension. These qualities are called the heavenly abodes (*brahmavihāras*) and consist of kindness (*mettā*), compassion (*karuṇā*), joy (*mudita*), and equanimity (*upekkhā*). This journey is not limited to just these four. Any state of mind-heart that feels expansive, light, or uplifted is fine.[6] But kindness is where this journey begins. Create phrases that resonate with this feeling: "May I be happy," "May I be peaceful," "May I have ease." No wholesome quality is necessarily better than any other. Use whatever works best for you and comes most easily and naturally.

Say the phrases sincerely with clear intention. Don't say them quickly or rapidly like a mantra or purposely coordinate them with the breath. Use one phrase, feel it, put that feeling in your heart, and stay with it as long as it lasts. When it fades, make another wish. There is nothing magic in the words themselves. It is the feeling that is most helpful.

If you have difficulty finding the feeling, smile. Shortly we'll explore the use of smiling in meditation. For now just know that smiling helps these qualities come more easily. This is a smiling meditation.

You send or wish these qualities to yourself because you cannot truly send to others what you don't already experience. In the West, many of us grew up

---

6 For example, generosity, peacefulness, love, gentleness, and gratitude have little tension and tend to reduce tension and suffering. They too are considered wholesome.

with attitudes of self-hatred we don't even recognize. Sending these qualities to ourselves helps soften and balance such unwholesome tendencies.

You send these qualities to your spiritual friend to cultivate a consciousness that extends beyond yourself. As you send uplifted energy to others, a personalized sense of self may feel less important. This impersonal nature of experience (*anattā*) is one of the basic characteristics of all things.

Joy

While radiating the feeling of loving kindness, there may be moments of joy (*pīti*)—soft bursts of well-being that have nothing to do with self or other. Your attention may be drawn there. It's very healing. As you relax into joy, it spreads out and softens into a quiet and comfortable feeling of happiness (*sukha*). As you relax into happiness, it may spread out into a more spacious peacefulness called "unification of mind-heart." This feeling may be so quiet that the mind loses contact with it.

This little cycle from joy to happiness to peacefulness may pass quickly—a little burst of well-being that fades. That's fine. With time and patience, it will lengthen on its own.

This cycle is where the meditation journey begins. It's a toe in the door. It draws and quiets the mind-heart. Don't hold onto it—holding creates tension. In the beginning it is easier to connect with this joy, kindness, or uplift than it is to sustain contact with it. But each time you contact it, the stability of mind-heart strengthens a bit. As you relax into this uplift, it will grow.

You may feel intense joy. Or it may be tentative and fleeting. Still you are on the path. As you relax into the joy, it may become more powerful. Then it passes. It always does.

> *He who binds to himself a joy*
> *Does the winged life destroy;*
> *But he who kisses the joy as it flies*
> *Lives in eternity's sunrise.*
> —William Blake

The Six Rs

The practice of sending loving-kindness or well-being is the storefront of this meditation. It is something wholesome to occupy the mind-heart in meditation and in daily life. There is a second aspect of this practice in the back room that is just as important—if not more important.

As you send well-wishing to yourself or your spiritual friend, other things will occur uninvited. Thoughts, images, sensations, and emotions will waltz in. That's not your intention. But the mind has a mind of its own.

As long as you're still with the well-wishing for yourself or your spiritual friend, this is not a problem. If thoughts don't pull the mind away from the kindness, joy or well-being, then ignore them. Let them float in the background, as it were.

But sooner or later, a distraction hijacks your attention completely. You won't see it coming: one moment you're sending loving-kindness, the next you're rehearsing a conversation, planning your day, reminiscing about yesterday, or attending to things other than the object of meditation.

Rejoice! Now you get to use the second part of the practice—a powerful technique that can only be used when the mind wanders. Now's your chance!

The drifting mind is a symptom of tension that is disturbing your underlying peace. This side of enlightenment, we all have many tensions. So the distraction points one out—it shows exactly where it is so that you can release it skillfully. This is good news.

The trick is to do it wisely! An unwise way is to condemn yourself, "Oh, I can't do this!" That criticism creates more tension and destabilizes the mind further. Another unwise strategy is to buckle down and try harder—a kind of greed for something different. This too creates more tension and restlessness.

A better approach is employing a six-phased process we affectionately call "the Six Rs."

Recognize that your attention has moved. Seeing how the mind's attention shifts from one thing to another is crucial. In time it will be clear that some wisdom drew you to that particular place. The reason may not be clear now. That's fine. If a thought drew you away, there's no need to get involved in the content. It's not important. If the content could awaken us, we would have become enlightened a long time ago. Instead, notice the feeling of the mind-heart. There will be some tension: worry, curiosity, aversion, fear, desire, doubt, or some other attitude. Recognizing this tightness is very helpful.

Release your grip on the distraction. Let it be. Don't push it away. Just release the hold it has on your attention.

Relax. Let go of any tension you feel in your mind or body. You don't have to search for tension like an enthusiastic detective. Just relax. That's enough.

Re-smile, or smile again. The smile may be on your lips, in your mind, in your eyes, or in your heart. If no uplifted state comes on its own, raise the corners of the mouth slightly. Even if you do this mechanically, it effectively encourages the mind to lighten up. Having a good sense of humor about how the mind drifts is helpful.

Return. Now take the relaxed mind-heart and this brighter and lighter state back to the object of meditation: sending happiness and well-being.

Repeat these steps each time the mind's attention wanders off. If you haven't released all the tension from a particular distraction, that's fine. It will come up again until you have. You can relax in the confidence that the mind-heart will let you know if there's more to relax.

The purpose of the Six Rs is not to get rid of something. It is to see it clearly, accept it as it is, release the tension in it, and then go back to radiating kindness or happiness. If you use the Six Rs to try and make a distraction go away, you are practicing aversion. This doesn't help!

The Six-R process is a practical implementation of Wise Effort (or "Right Effort"), the fourth step of the Buddha's Eightfold Path. And the Eightfold Path is the fourth of the Buddha's Four Ennobling Truths. In practicing this way you are engaging the Buddha's core teachings.

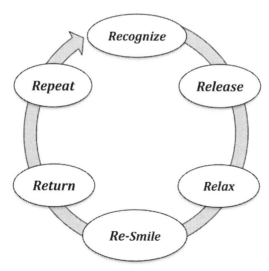

Continuity

Thirty minutes a day of meditation is adequate to start. Forty-five minutes is better. When the meditation goes well, allow it to extend longer. Twice a day is better yet. The best results come when you can relax and sit without moving. If the mind insists that you move, Six-R the insistence. The Six Rs are very helpful in letting the mind release tension and find deeper ease.

Of course, if pain arises from genuine physical harm, please adjust your posture. You can tell if the pain is genuine when you get up from sitting. If the hurt goes away quickly, it was not caused by anything harmful. If that discomfort returns when you sit next time, remain still and Six-R. On the other hand, if the pain lingers when you get up, there is a physical problem. It is best not to sit that way in the future.

Meditation and its benefits increase when you smile throughout the day. Send kindness and happiness whenever you think of it. And when you notice difficult feelings, Six-R them. If you push yourself to do this, you will wear out. So smile lightly and radiate kindness to those around you as often as you remember.

Impersonal

As you engage in meditation, it helps to understand how the process works. This is not a substitute for direct experience. But understanding helps you know what to look for and what to ignore. After all, the first aspect of the Buddha's Eightfold Path is Wise View (also known as "Right Understanding").

The most important aspect of Wise View is the impersonal nature of all phenomena. Even some of the ways we tend to think and feel were probably shaped by impersonal natural selection.

Our evolutionary ancestors had soft, vulnerable bodies. They didn't have the strength of a bear, the claws of a lion, the teeth of a wolf, or the shells of a turtle. To survive they used their wits. They were scavengers who learned to analyze and adapt to changing threats and opportunities. They learned to think in complex ways.

They had instincts, but they had more mental and fewer behavioral instincts. One instinct focused attention quickly and tightly on anything that helped them survive (e.g., food) and anything that threatened their existence (e.g., predators). And it helped them ignore anything that was not relevant to survival or procreation. Today Buddhists call these three aspects of this instinct desire, aversion, and ignorance.

Another instinct was the urge to play and explore their surroundings and to remember what they discovered. This helped them adjust more rapidly to changing circumstances. Today we call this instinct curiosity and wandering mind.

Even the instinct to take things personally arose out of impersonal contingencies. Those who were at peace with living and dying were less likely to pass their DNA along than those obsessed with "me," "myself," and "my organism."

The Buddha didn't talk about evolution or natural selection. But he did say that "me, myself, and mine" represent ignorance and delusion. When we observe with relaxed, clear awareness, there is no me, myself, or mine. There are thoughts, feelings, and sensations. The mind calls them "my thoughts," "my feelings," and "my sensations." The "my" is tagged on by the mind. It's not in the actual experience.

Apparently our ancestors were successful. Today we are no longer a marginal species: we are the top of the food chain. We've subdued or wiped out most creatures that threaten us. The only significant danger left is ourselves. But we still carry the genes and neural wiring bred into us by millions of years of evolution.

When we sit down to meditate and find thoughts racing like hamsters on caffeine, the mind is doing what it was designed to do. It's not personal. Ruminating over old wounds, rehearsing future conversations, creating to-do lists, anticipating trips, and other kinds of planning, fixing, figuring, personalizing, and thinking are by-products of evolutionary tendencies. The mind is simply doing its job. Greed, hatred, and delusion aren't moral failings: they are leftovers of natural selection. And since we've been acting on these urges all our lives, the mind is also doing what we trained it to do.

Desire, greed, aversion, anger, personalizing, and other dense or agitated states are impersonal phenomena to be observed rather than personal failings to be atoned for. They are complex biological reflexes that helped us survive when we were marginal fauna. But they don't help us thrive now that we are dominant. We are not responsible for the evolutionary forces that bred these tendencies into us. They are the cards we were dealt. But we are responsible for how we play those cards today. We are responsible for how we respond to those qualities in the mind-heart. Unwholesome qualities like craving, clinging, and personalizing distort thinking, perception, and judgment. They may cause us to bring suffering into our lives and strife into the world.

If we want to thrive and deepen well-being, we must relate to these unwholesome qualities with wisdom and clarity—this is to say, we must learn to Recognize, Release, Relax, Re-smile, Return to the wholesome, and Repeat as needed. And at the same time we must cultivate other wholesome qualities—ones that have little tension or distortion in them.

The rabbi came to the altar and began beating his chest, "I'm nobody, I'm nobody, I'm nobody."

The cantor knelt down next to the rabbi and beat his chest, "I'm nobody, I'm nobody, I'm nobody."

The janitor saw them, knelt down, and began beating his chest, "I'm nobody, I'm nobody, I'm nobody."

The cantor turned to the rabbi and said, "Look who thinks he's nobody."

Awareness Is Magic

The most important wholesome quality we can cultivate may be ease. Busy mind, desire, aversion, and spacing out are triggered by external and internal stressors. Stress distorts our attention by focusing on things around us that we want or don't want. This is why the Release, Relax, and Re-smile steps are so valuable: they allow distorting tension to relax. They help our awareness unglue from what's "out there" and drift inward to see what's actually going on "in here." The entire practice is about becoming lighter, happier, and more accepting no matter what is going on "out there."

Pure awareness has a seemingly magical calming effect. "Pure" means awareness with no tension, no distortion, and no agenda. It sees without judgment. If we're mindful, we can feel how awareness works:

- If the mind-heart is restless, depressed, irritated, or worried and we observe it without preference, it calms down. But if we have the slightest aversion or desire for it to be different, thoughts run amuck and feelings intensify.

- Similarly, if we're calm or joyful but aren't aware of it, our mood tends to tighten. But if we are serene and know it, the serenity deepens.[7]

---

7 For example, when we take a bite of chocolate, the mind may become joyful and serene because the hunger for chocolate is suddenly gone. If we relax into the good feeling, it gets stronger. But if we think the bliss was created by the chocolate itself, we quickly reach for more. In that greed, the serenity is disturbed.

Pure awareness has this uplifting effect when we remember to observe awareness itself. So this practice begins by cultivating wholesome qualities like kindness, compassion, peace, and joy and sending those out. And when unwholesome qualities enter the mind-heart like stress, desire, fear, or the urge to numb out, it helps to see them impersonally. They aren't ethical failures, just evolutionary residues.

Rather than focus on the content of the thoughts or on situations out there, we can observe the unwholesome qualities without preference. We just see them as they are without trying to change them (Recognize and Release). We view with detached interest.

If we try to get rid of unpleasant qualities, we just add more greed and aversion to the mind-heart. However, if we know them openly and objectively, we view the unwholesome qualities with wholesome awareness. This pure, clear awareness gradually melts disturbing attitudes.

To walk the Buddha's path, we don't try to control the mind-heart. We observe how the mind's attention moves from object to object. We notice qualities of awareness. We Six-R unwholesome states. We gently and continuously cultivate awareness of awareness.

The Great Way is not difficult for those who have no preferences. Without desire and hate, everything becomes clear and undisguised. If you want to see the truth, then hold no opinion for or against anything. Make the slightest distinction and heaven and earth are set infinitely apart.

—Sengstan

Buddha's Map

As your meditation settles in, you move along the path the Buddha mapped out more than two and a half millennia ago. He did not create this path. He discovered it and charted it. It is a natural unfolding of the heart-mind.

The booklet *Mettā-Paññā*[8] gives a short overview of this path in its entirety. The book *Buddha's Map*[9] provides a detailed field guide with stories, images, and experiences that help you recognize where you are and know where to explore next.

If you have another kind of meditation practice, I encourage you to give this approach a try. Or at least insert a Relax step into how you deal with distractions: when your mind wanders, rather than pulling your attention immediately back to your object of meditation, relax first.

The Buddha saw that craving (or tightness) and personalizing are the roots of suffering and distractions. Relaxing the tightness goes to the core of his teaching and practice. This simple step can make a huge difference. So give it a try. And if you find that helpful, try all six Rs.

---

8 Doug Kraft, *Mettā-Paññā: A Quick Guide to Kindness and Wisdom Meditation* (Blue Dolphin Publishing, 2014).

9 Kraft, *Buddha's Map: His Original Teachings on Awakening, Ease, and Insight in the Heart of Meditation* (Blue Dolphin Publishing, 2013).

Teaspoon of Salt

An old proverb says that if we stir a teaspoon of salt into a glass of water, it makes the water so bitter it's undrinkable. However, if we stir it into a five-gallon cistern, we don't even notice the salt.

Life has its salt: discomforts, suffering, and dissatisfaction. Trying to get rid of them is futile. However, we can become larger containers. By sending mettā, we allow ourselves to expand. By releasing, relaxing, and smiling, we become more spacious. As we do so, we are walking the Buddha's path of kindness and wisdom.

May all beings be happy.
May all beings have ease as they walk through their day.
May all beings know their true nature.

Resources

Bhante Vimalaraṁsi, *Breath of Love* (Ehipassiko Foundation of Indonesia, 2012).

———, *Moving Dhamma, Volume 1.* (Dhamma Sukha Meditation Center, 2012).

Dhamma Sukha Meditation Center website: http://www.dhammasukha.org.

Doug Kraft, *Buddha's Map: His Original Teachings on Awakening, Ease, and Insight in the Heart of Meditation* (Blue Dolphin Publishing, 2013).

———, *Circling Home: Spirituality Through a Unitarian Universalist Lens* (CreateSpace, 2010).

———, *God(s) and Consciousness: Mapping the Development of Consciousness Through Views of Ultimacy* (Doug Kraft Books, 2011).

———, *Mettā-Paññā: A Quick Guide to Kindness and Wisdom Meditation* (Blue Dolphin Publishing, 2014).

Easing Awake website: http://www.dougkraft.com.

Sayadaw U Tejaniya, *Don't Look Down on Defilements*, (Auspicious Affinity, 2006), http://www.sayadawutejaniya.org.

———, *Dhamma Everywhere*, (Auspicious Affinity, 2011), http://www.sayadawutejaniya.org.

———, *Awareness Alone Is Not Enough*, (Auspicious Affinity, 2008), http://www.sayadawutejaniya.org.